This book belongs to

....

....

Date:...................

Today I am grateful for...

_____

_____

_____

_____

_____

_____

Something awesome that happened today was...

_____

_____

_____

_____

_____

_____

_____

MY HAPPINESS SCALE

10
9
8
7
6
5
4
3
2
1

Date:.................

Today I am grateful for...

Something awesome that happened today was...

MY HAPPINESS SCALE

10
9
8
7
6
5
4
3
2
1

Date:...................

Today I am grateful for...

_____
_____
_____
_____
_____
_____
_____
_____

Something awesome that happened today was...

_____
_____
_____
_____
_____
_____
_____
_____

MY HAPPINESS SCALE

10
9
8
7
6
5
4
3
2
1

Date:..................

Today I am grateful for...

Something awesome that happened today was...

MY HAPPINESS SCALE

10
9
8
7
6
5
4
3
2
1

Date:...................

Today I am grateful for...

Something awesome that happened today was...

MY HAPPINESS SCALE

10
9
8
7
6
5
4
3
2
1

Date:..................

Today I am grateful for...

Something awesome that happened today was...

MY HAPPINESS SCALE

10
9
8
7
6
5
4
3
2
1

Date:....................

Today I am grateful for...

Something awesome that happened today was...

MY HAPPINESS SCALE

10
9
8
7
6
5
4
3
2
1

Date:..................

Today I am grateful for...

Something awesome that happened today was...

MY HAPPINESS SCALE

10
9
8
7
6
5
4
3
2
1

Date:....................

Today I am grateful for...

_____

_____

_____

_____

_____

_____

MY HAPPINESS SCALE

Something awesome that
happened today was...

_____

_____

_____

_____

_____

_____

_____

10
9
8
7
6
5
4
3
2
1

Date:..................

Today I am grateful for...

_____
_____
_____
_____
_____
_____
_____

Something awesome that happened today was...

_____
_____
_____
_____
_____
_____

MY HAPPINESS SCALE

10
9
8
7
6
5
4
3
2
1

Date:.................

Today I am grateful for...

Something awesome that happened today was...

MY HAPPINESS SCALE

10
9
8
7
6
5
4
3
2
1

Date:...................

Today I am grateful for...

Something awesome that happened today was...

MY HAPPINESS SCALE

10
9
8
7
6
5
4
3
2
1

Date:.................

Today I am grateful for...

Something awesome that happened today was...

MY HAPPINESS SCALE

10
9
8
7
6
5
4
3
2
1

Date:....................

Today I am grateful for...

Something awesome that happened today was...

MY HAPPINESS SCALE

10
9
8
7
6
5
4
3
2
1

Date:..................

Today I am grateful for...

Something awesome that happened today was...

MY HAPPINESS SCALE

10
9
8
7
6
5
4
3
2
1

Date:..................

Today I am grateful for...

Something awesome that happened today was...

MY HAPPINESS SCALE

10
9
8
7
6
5
4
3
2
1

Date:...................

Today I am grateful for...

Something awesome that happened today was...

MY HAPPINESS SCALE

10
9
8
7
6
5
4
3
2
1

Date:..................

Today I am grateful for...

Something awesome that happened today was...

MY HAPPINESS SCALE

10
9
8
7
6
5
4
3
2
1

Date:...................

Today I am grateful for...

Something awesome that happened today was...

MY HAPPINESS SCALE

10
9
8
7
6
5
4
3
2
1

Date:...................

Today I am grateful for...

Something awesome that happened today was...

MY HAPPINESS SCALE

10
9
8
7
6
5
4
3
2
1

Date:..................

Today I am grateful for...

Something awesome that happened today was...

MY HAPPINESS SCALE

10
9
8
7
6
5
4
3
2
1

Date:..................

Today I am grateful for...

Something awesome that happened today was...

MY HAPPINESS SCALE

10
9
8
7
6
5
4
3
2
1

Date:...................

Today I am grateful for...

Something awesome that happened today was...

MY HAPPINESS SCALE

10
9
8
7
6
5
4
3
2
1

Date:..................

Today I am grateful for...

_____
_____
_____
_____
_____
_____
_____

Something awesome that happened today was...

_____
_____
_____
_____
_____
_____
_____
_____

MY HAPPINESS SCALE

10
9
8
7
6
5
4
3
2
1

Date:..................

Today I am grateful for...

_____
_____
_____
_____
_____
_____
_____
_____

Something awesome that happened today was...

_____
_____
_____
_____
_____
_____
_____
_____

MY HAPPINESS SCALE

10
9
8
7
6
5
4
3
2
1

Date:...................

Today I am grateful for...

_____
_____
_____
_____
_____
_____
_____
_____

Something awesome that happened today was...

_____
_____
_____
_____
_____
_____
_____
_____

MY HAPPINESS SCALE

10
9
8
7
6
5
4
3
2
1

Date:...................

Today I am grateful for...

Something awesome that happened today was...

MY HAPPINESS SCALE

10
9
8
7
6
5
4
3
2
1

Date:...................

Today I am grateful for...

Something awesome that happened today was...

MY HAPPINESS SCALE

10
9
8
7
6
5
4
3
2
1

Date:....................

Today I am grateful for...

_____
_____
_____
_____
_____
_____
_____

Something awesome that happened today was...

_____
_____
_____
_____
_____
_____
_____

MY HAPPINESS SCALE

10
9
8
7
6
5
4
3
2
1

Date:....................

Today I am grateful for...

Something awesome that happened today was...

MY HAPPINESS SCALE

10
9
8
7
6
5
4
3
2
1

Date:...................

Today I am grateful for...

Something awesome that happened today was...

MY HAPPINESS SCALE

10
9
8
7
6
5
4
3
2
1

Date:...................

Today I am grateful for...

Something awesome that happened today was...

MY HAPPINESS SCALE

10
9
8
7
6
5
4
3
2
1

Date:....................

Today I am grateful for...

Something awesome that happened today was...

MY HAPPINESS SCALE

10
9
8
7
6
5
4
3
2
1

Date:....................

Today I am grateful for...

_____
_____
_____
_____
_____
_____
_____

Something awesome that happened today was...

_____
_____
_____
_____
_____
_____
_____
_____
_____

MY HAPPINESS SCALE

10
9
8
7
6
5
4
3
2
1

Date:..................

Today I am grateful for...

_____
_____
_____
_____
_____
_____
_____
_____

Something awesome that happened today was...

_____
_____
_____
_____
_____
_____
_____
_____

MY HAPPINESS SCALE

10
9
8
7
6
5
4
3
2
1

Date:..................

Today I am grateful for...

Something awesome that happened today was...

MY HAPPINESS SCALE

10
9
8
7
6
5
4
3
2
1

Date:...................

Today I am grateful for...

Something awesome that happened today was...

MY HAPPINESS SCALE

10
9
8
7
6
5
4
3
2
1

Date:....................

Today I am grateful for...

Something awesome that happened today was...

MY HAPPINESS SCALE

10
9
8
7
6
5
4
3
2
1

Date:...................

Today I am grateful for...

Something awesome that happened today was...

MY HAPPINESS SCALE

10
9
8
7
6
5
4
3
2
1

Date:...................

Today I am grateful for...

Something awesome that happened today was...

MY HAPPINESS SCALE

10
9
8
7
6
5
4
3
2
1

Date:....................

Today I am grateful for...

Something awesome that happened today was...

MY HAPPINESS SCALE

10
9
8
7
6
5
4
3
2
1

Date:...................

Today I am grateful for...

_____
_____
_____
_____
_____
_____
_____

Something awesome that happened today was...

_____
_____
_____
_____
_____
_____
_____
_____

MY HAPPINESS SCALE

10
9
8
7
6
5
4
3
2
1

Date:....................

Today I am grateful for...

Something awesome that happened today was...

MY HAPPINESS SCALE

10
9
8
7
6
5
4
3
2
1

Date:..................

Today I am grateful for...

Something awesome that happened today was...

MY HAPPINESS SCALE

10
9
8
7
6
5
4
3
2
1

Date:....................

Today I am grateful for...

Something awesome that happened today was...

MY HAPPINESS SCALE

10
9
8
7
6
5
4
3
2
1

Date:..................

Today I am grateful for...

Something awesome that happened today was...

MY HAPPINESS SCALE

10
9
8
7
6
5
4
3
2
1

Date:..................

Today I am grateful for...

Something awesome that happened today was...

MY HAPPINESS SCALE

10
9
8
7
6
5
4
3
2
1

Date:..................

Today I am grateful for...

Something awesome that happened today was...

MY HAPPINESS SCALE

10
9
8
7
6
5
4
3
2
1

Date:....................

Today I am grateful for...

Something awesome that happened today was...

MY HAPPINESS SCALE

10
9
8
7
6
5
4
3
2
1

Date:..................

Today I am grateful for...

Something awesome that happened today was...

MY HAPPINESS SCALE

10
9
8
7
6
5
4
3
2
1

Date:.................

Today I am grateful for...

Something awesome that happened today was...

MY HAPPINESS SCALE

10
9
8
7
6
5
4
3
2
1

Date:.................

Today I am grateful for...

Something awesome that happened today was...

MY HAPPINESS SCALE

10
9
8
7
6
5
4
3
2
1

Date:....................

Today I am grateful for...

Something awesome that happened today was...

MY HAPPINESS SCALE

10
9
8
7
6
5
4
3
2
1

Date:..................

Today I am grateful for...

Something awesome that happened today was...

MY HAPPINESS SCALE

10
9
8
7
6
5
4
3
2
1

Date:..................

Today I am grateful for...

_____

_____

_____

_____

_____

_____

_____

Something awesome that
happened today was...

_____

_____

_____

_____

_____

_____

_____

_____

MY HAPPINESS SCALE

10
9
8
7
6
5
4
3
2
1

Date:.................

Today I am grateful for...

MY HAPPINESS SCALE

Something awesome that happened today was...

10
9
8
7
6
5
4
3
2
1

Date:..................

Today I am grateful for...

Something awesome that happened today was...

MY HAPPINESS SCALE

10
9
8
7
6
5
4
3
2
1

Date:.................

Today I am grateful for...

Something awesome that happened today was...

MY HAPPINESS SCALE

10
9
8
7
6
5
4
3
2
1

Date:....................

Today I am grateful for...

_____

_____

_____

_____

_____

_____

_____

Something awesome that
happened today was...

_____

_____

_____

_____

_____

_____

_____

_____

_____

MY HAPPINESS SCALE

10
9
8
7
6
5
4
3
2
1

Date:..................

Today I am grateful for...

Something awesome that happened today was...

MY HAPPINESS SCALE

10
9
8
7
6
5
4
3
2
1

Made in the USA
Lexington, KY
26 October 2018